LOGOS
The Development of Visual Symbols

Steven Skaggs

CRISP PUBLICATIONS, INC.
Menlo Park, California

LOGOS
The Development of Visual Symbols

Steven Skaggs

CREDITS:
Editor: **Kay Kepler**
Typesetting: **Execustaff**
Cover Design: **Execustaff**
Artwork: **Steven Skaggs**

The BIOS logo appearing on page 123 is for the exclusive use of The BIOS Foundation and the Medical Wellness Center of the Maritimes and appears here through their courtesy.

The appearance of the devises, logos, or trademarks that appear here are for the sole purpose of illustrating the educational themes of this book.

Library of Congress Catalog Card Number 92-54358
Skaggs, Steven
Logos
ISBN 0-56052-189-9

Contents

I. Beginning Sketches
Searching for the Mobius Yin-Yang

THE BUZZ of the telephone interrupted my grading.

"Professor Skaggs?" The voice was crisp, young. "This is Dr. Will LaValley. I'm calling to see if you could possibly help me with a logo.

Actually, I already know what I need. It's just a simple matter of drawing it for me."

It was time to bail out of this conversation as fast as I tactfully could and get back to grading the projects. "I'm sorry, Dr. LaValley, but I'm afraid you've come to the wrong place. You need someone who does technical drawing, drafting, production art. I'd be happy to supply you with some names."

Little did I know that this was the beginning of a very rewarding exploration into the process of design—a project that would be unusual in that the client was allowed behind the scenes to witness the unfolding of concepts, the investigation of each idea, the refinement of chosen directions and the drawing of master art.

He insisted. "I'm told that you specialize in logo design. I've got a new organization that really needs a drawing that combines a yin-yang with a Mobius strip. It's just a matter of working it out."

I was intrigued by two things. One was the game of trying to combine a yin-yang and a Mobius strip. The other was a nagging curiousity about what this guy might be doing that would cause him to need two arcane objects such as these.

"Let's back up a bit. Why don't you start from the top and explain what you're up to here?"

An M.D. fresh from Houston doing his residency at a local hospital, LaValley had entered into a partnership with a doctor from Nova Scotia to begin a nonprofit foundation named BIOS. The foundation was to encourage research on non-Western medical practices such as acupuncture, herbal treatments, homeopathic remedies. Could Western research methods discover reasons for the apparent effectiveness of some of these practices? If so, then bringing the principles of some of these folk remedies into mainstream medicine would open new vistas for future Western medical development. These were truly ambitious goals.

In our conversation, it was clear that although LaValley thought the yin-yang and Mobius strip were natural devices to symbolize the union of Eastern and Western philosophies, he was open to the exploration of alternatives. I agreed with him—these did seem to be apt symbols. We decided to have a meeting at which I would try to gain a fuller understanding of the new foundation and he would get a sense of my design methodology.

It is important to have a face-to-face meeting with someone to understand their concerns. This is one reason why, no matter how spatially dispersed and independent computer networks may allow us to become, meetings are always necessary. The Will LaValley with whom I spoke on the phone seemed interested only in the end product and getting there as quickly as possible. But in the flesh, Will LaValley struck me as someone who was interested in the journey, not just the destination. As we talked, our conversation ranged over a wide group of topics: chaos theory; the seeming impossibility of homeopathic effects; concepts from particle physics that may account for the ultimate validation of homeopathy; baseball. In the process, I gained an appreciation for Will. I began to see him as someone truly interested in and excited by ideas. I could see how this interest would lead him to begin something like the BIOS Foundation, and I began to share his enthusiasm for the prospect of applying scientific method to traditional folk remedies.

After an explanation of the nature of graphic design, Will LaValley, in turn, became increasingly interested in the notion of developing from scratch a visual identifier for BIOS. He especially wanted to know precisely what course the ideas might take. Perhaps there could be more appropriate symbols than the yin-yang/Mobius strip. But what kind of ideas might these be and how might they relate to one another? He needed to know the course the ideas might take.

We agreed on an unusual program. In return for the freedom to go where the project seemed to want to go, I would reveal to him the lines of thought as they stretched toward what we both hoped would be a very appropriate emblem for the BIOS Foundation. He risked spending a lot of money for something no more useful than his original idea. I risked spending a lot of time on a project that would end up a quagmire of

inconclusive sketches. To keep control of this project, and to keep it from becoming a nightmare for either of us, we agreed that the work would be presented in stages. I would work on it for about a week, then meet with Will and show a group of sketches. In response to that critique, I would develop another set of sketches, meet again to further develop the direction, and continue in this manner until the design was resolved.

With my marching orders, I returned to the studio. Among my first sketches was a series of yin-yang/Mobius strips.

Overview

THE GENERAL public has become very aware of the significance of visual symbols, especially those used as trademarks. Visual symbols of every form imaginable are used as elements in fashion, flaunted in commercials for consumer products, even (in the case of the MTV logo) made into a cartoon character. Logos are no longer subliminal devices that simply "mark" the maker of merchandise. They have become a kind of decorative functionary in a social context.

Marks are often compared to suits of clothes. The claim is made that just as it is important for the business executive to "dress for success," so it is important that the logo look professional. This analogy is shallow. It places a logo in the superficial role of being fashionable—an object of aesthetics. A logo serves a function that is at once more humble and more permanent. A logo is a visual name, a moniker. This modest function allows communication to take place "in the name of" the host. The ad, the brochure and the video commercial act as surrogates. The logo implicitly says, "This message is brought to you by . . ." In this manner, a logo is more like a face than it is like a suit of clothes. It is the face a company presents, not only to the public, but to its employees and to itself. To look into a person's eyes is to gain more information about a person's character than to notice a suit of clothes. The logo assumes the task of representing the core forces that shape a company's vision, the visual representation of the host philosophy and attitudes.

A second misconception is that a logo is the visual image of a company, or that a corporate identity and logo are synonymous. A logo is only a *small part* of the visual image of a company. Applications of the mark on everything from letterheads to packaging, the general design of communications emanating from the company, the architecture and interior design of the company's buildings—all of these play a vital role in determining the visual image.

The corporate image comes from corporate behavior as well as visual presentation. In a well-planned system, each of these interrelated parts will be sensitive to each other. The result is an organizational character in which, one hopes, the public acquires a firm, uncontradicted sense of the corporate philosophy and sees that philosophy in action through consistent corporate behavior. The logo is capable of sending messages about the philosophy and of being a receptacle for the image of the company as projected through corporate behavior. Paul Rand once said (*Artograph* No. 6) that his design of the IBM logo was meant to be distinctive; it was only after a few years that the horizontal lines began to take on the meaning "high tech" through the association with IBM's products and services.

So the primary role of the logo is twofold. It must identify the host, and it must send the right feelings and connotations in the process. This game is a classic one, as old as our species, and a challenging one. Working on a logo is a journey through a labyrinth, a maze of possible directions to take, of decision points. It is a fascinating journey, with many potential solutions, but many more pitfalls and hazards. No two games will ever present identical challenges, nor will the road to the chosen solution be traveled twice. Designers walk into the game with their eyes wide open, ready for the unexpected, because the unexpected can be expected to occur. To walk into that first meeting with the client is to accept the quest. The game begins.

Note: Each logo sketch illustrated on the following pages carries two kinds of numbers. The inventory number *is a three digit code that indicates the chronological sequence in which the logo was sketched. The illustrations are arranged on the page by this chronological sequence.*

The second number is the protocol diagram number. *A protocol is a series of steps performed to reach some goal. The protocol diagram in the Appendix makes it possible to map the relationships of one idea or concept to others. During the course of the BIOS project, thirty-one different concepts were explored. Each of these concepts is assigned a number from one to thirty-one. A decimal system has also been employed to pinpoint sketches within each conceptual series. The sketch carrying protocol number 3.10 for example, is part of the third concept series and is the tenth version (or iteration) of the concept.*

BIOS is a word that cries out to be seen. It is short, distinctive and suggests the nature of the foundation's activities. Because the BIOS Foundation has little in the way of a promotional campaign, the name must be easily remembered. Logos that use entire names rather than abstract ideograms or pictographic icons are called logotypes; to build name recognition, a logotype is a reasonable solution for BIOS.

It is not sufficient for a logotype to be the simple typographic rendering of a word. Logotypes, as do all logos, must act as distinctive and memorable emblems. Something about the BIOS logotype must carve out a place for itself in the buzz of visual symbols that stream past viewers, something that sets the logotype apart from generic typeset words. Stressing of the long 'O,' even marking the 'O' by

Sketch 001(1.1) Sketch 002(1.2) Sketch 003(1.3) Sketch 004(1.4)

Johnston BIOS   *Gramercy* BIOS   *perpetua* BIOS   *Gill Sans* BIOS

Sketch 005(1.5) Sketch 006(1.6) Sketch 007(1.7) Sketch 008(1.8)

BIOS   BIOS   BIOS   **BIOS**

placing a diacritical mark, presents the opportunity of replacing the circular 'O' with some similarly shaped symbolic device that can convey a sense of the foundation's mission. Deciding to pursue a logotype that uses a symbol in place of one of the characters does not narrow the scope of the study; it simply provides a focus for work, a welcome center of gravity for the unfolding investigation.

Sketches 1–9: The first step is simply to see what the word B I O S looks like. Different typefaces give a sense of the possible range of feelings provoked by the four letters. The typefaces are conservative in form and weight. The idea is not to look upon them as serious candidates for the final design, but simply to gauge the rhythms and contrasts of the letterforms.

BIOS

Sketch 10: This shape will be a yin-yang emblem when it is vertically oriented, but rotated to a horizontal position it can also be seen as a sine wave. Both interpretations have a favorable resonance with the mission of the foundation.

Sketch 11: This is what a Mobius strip might look like as a drawing. It must be placed horizontally or it reads as the figure eight.

The idea of combining the yin-yang and the Mobius strip into one form remains enticing; but how can it be done? The twisting shape of the strip could be made to trace the lines of the yin-yang. The difficulty lies in reconciling the breadth of the strip with the necessity for yin and yang to meet along an edge. A second problem is the need of the yin-yang to appear with black and white countercharging. It is not easy to introduce this requirement into the concept of the Mobius, as the overly complex sketch 15 illustrates. The yet-more-complex sketch 16, with its retained black disk, is on the verge of losing any sense of unity.

Sketch 017(3.7)

Sketch 018(3.8)

Sketch 019(3.9)

Sketch 020(3.10)

Whenever sketches become too complex or stuffed with information, it is always a good idea to step back and recover aspects of the form that seem to be successful. This happens in sketch 18 where yin, yang and circle are momentarily forgotten and the Mobius attains a higher sense of order and movement.

The small sketches 19, 20 and 21 chart the attempt to restore yin and yang. The goal of blending both Mobius and yin-yang is almost realized, although neither is easy to see—one might as easily see two tadpoles.

This line of investigation reaches a momentary conclusion in the larger sketches 22 and 23. Eliminating some of the pictorial qualities of the earlier sketch diminishes recognition of the objects, but the emblem is more dynamic, memorable and unified. The question evolves: How important is it that the viewer recognize yin, yang, Mobius?

Sketch 24 is an attempt to see if the thin lines forming the back surface of the Mobius strip can be removed. This step shows that the Mobius strip is now completely lost. Since the unity and dynamic qualities of the symbol are not improved, this idea is not pursued further.

15

Sketch 025(3.15)

Sketch 026(3A.16)

Sketch 027(3B.16)

Sketch 028(3A.17)

16

Sketch 25: What happens if the Mobius strip alone could become easier to identify? The strip is given dimension by the addition of gradient lines. The added sense of shading helps the Mobius strip to appear as a three-dimensional form. The line above the symbol is the first indication that the symbol is intended to replace the 'O' in the foundation's name. The line serves as a diacritical mark to ensure the correct pronunciation (the title of the foundation was officially registered with the diacritical mark in place). Although sketch 25 is easy to see as a strip and also recalls the symbol for infinity, the formation of the emblem is awkward. The oblong shape would be simplified and more rational if it could become a circle. The gradient lines look too much like a woodcut, carrying connotations of medieval times. The look

Sketch 029(3B.17)

Sketch 030(3B.18)

Sketch 031(3B.19)

Sketch 032(3B.20)

should be very contemporary and carry a sense of Western technology.

 Sketches 26–46: A series of 20 sketches explores the possibility of a Mobius strip inscribed in a circle or disk. The first challenge is to find a way to reconcile the verticality of the edges of the strip with the arc of the circle. The problems are readily apparent in sketches 27 and 29, where there is tension on the left and right sides of the mark. The next 17 sketches represent attempts to solve this problem. If the circle becomes the strip, by interacting with it in sketch 30, the emblem becomes lopsided.

 Sketch 31 brings the mark back into balance, but at the expense of clarity on the sides. How should these sides make the bend into the interior? Sketch 32 tests line weight and discovers that the thicker the line,

Sketch 033(3B.21)	*Sketch 034(3B.22)*	*Sketch 035(3B.23)*	*Sketch 036(3B.24)*

the more difficult it will become to make the transition clear. Sketches 33 and 34 define the transition better, but the emblem begins to look like an 'S'.

Sketch 35 is a module for testing qualities of the emblem. The next four sketches fail to overcome the problems of balance and clarity.

Note: *Occasionally, a series divides into branches that are distinctly different investigations of the same basic concept. Branches are indicated by letters within the protocol diagram number. The sketch carrying protocol number 24.B4 is the fourth iteration of branch B within concept series twenty-four. Continue to refer to the diagram in the Appendix to see the relationships of the conceptual series.*

Sketches 40, 41 and 42 abandon this line of thinking, looking back to earlier thoughts and attempting to introduce the quality of interaction of outside and inside in a different way.

Sketches 43 and 44 explore further possibilities, but the problems of indistinctness of the transitional curves return. The tangle of sketch 45 bears little resemblance to a Mobius strip, but the yin-yang returns. With sketch 46, a new concept emerges that suggests the traditional vertical yin-yang as well as a twisting strip (although not a Mobius strip). This emblem has a real sense of elegance and

Sketch 045(3B.30)	*Sketch 046(3B.31)*	*Sketch 047(4.1)*	*Sketch 048(4.2)*
		BIOS	BIOS

Sketch 049(4.3)	*Sketch 050(4.4)*	*Sketch 051(4.5)*	*Sketch 052(4.6)*
BIOS	BIOS	BIOS	BIOS

formality while containing a memorable optical illusion. However, it suggests an 'S' too strongly and it does not resemble a Mobius strip or a yin-yang closely enough to be seen as either.

Sketches 47–77: The sketches turn to investigations of the logotype with various designs inserted. Some modifications are made to some of the designs; for instance, sketches 53 and 63 hint at a new way to indicate continuity of line with an emphasis on the unity of style between the logotype and the ideograph.

Sketch 053(4A.7)

Sketch 054(4A.8)

Sketch 055(4A.9)

Sketch 056(4A.10)

Sketch 057(4A.11)

Sketch 058(4A.12)

Sketch 059(4A.13)

Sketch 060(4A.14)

Sketch 061(4A.15)

Sketch 062(4A.16)

Sketch 063(4A.17)

Sketch 064(4A.18)

Sketch 065(4B.7)

Sketch 066(4B.8)

Sketch 067(4B.9)

Sketch 068(4B.10)

How should the diacritical marking be handled? Should the typography be distinctive, or would that compete with the ideograph? How might the weights and line widths be balanced to provide a harmonious whole?

The nine sketches beginning with 69 are based on the design first rendered in sketches 21, 22 and 23. This development indicates that there is a preference for that design. It is simple, memorable and suggestive of the yin-yang and Mobius. It provides a catchy optical illusion in the manner in which background flows through the disk. The final sketch, 77, shows an interest in a minimalistic letterform

BIΞS

(somewhat archaic or primitive) combined with a Mobius reversed out of a black background. The emboldened ideograph is made slightly smaller, allowing a lowered, less conspicuous diacritical mark.

The first potential solution has been reached. But these efforts have all been traced along one narrow conceptual path—the union of Mobius and yin-yang. What directions could be found if the scope of the problem were broadened beyond Will LaValley's original intent?

The problem needs to unfold anew. It is time to put aside yin-yang and Mobius to find a new set of metaphors for the BIOS Foundation.

II. Particles from Waves
Stages of the Design Process

WILL AND I met at his apartment, where I explained what I had done. After the week's foray into BIOS territory, I thought I had made certain discoveries. My concern was that he understand that in order for the mark to be useful, it had to be simplified. I also wanted to check whether he agreed with my feeling that he needed to have the entire word BIOS stated. I emphasized that his audience must become aware of the foundation's name, but that it might be possible to include an emblem in place of the 'O'.

Will was intrigued with the sketches. He had no idea what a Mobius strip combined with a yin-yang might look like and seemed to be fascinated by the permutations. I described the main lines of thought. He responded right away to the marks that gave an illusion of depth (14, 18, 28), yet he agreed with me that the mark would need to be very simple and that 22 and 23 were nicely balanced, yet active.

These concepts were interesting, but I explained to Will that I thought these sketches just scratched the surface of possible concepts. I asked to do more sketches, aiming for a greater range of interpretation. He agreed that I should explore some more ideas—concepts that were not necessarily linked to yin-yang and Mobius.

Then he gave me a more detailed briefing about the interests of the BIOS Foundation. He described folk remedies from South America, acupuncture from China, and homeopathy (a practice that purports to cure "like with like" in extremely diluted form). BIOS would like to help support the study of these practices, he explained.

He argued cogently for the need to bring Western scientific methods to bear on these and other folk remedies. BIOS would not take a position on the effectiveness of any practice, but would try to stimulate interest among researchers to explore and explain folk remedies from the standpoint of the Western medical tradition.

With this discussion clearly focused in mind, I headed back to my car thinking about what kind of Western metaphors might be appropriate. Nuclear physics, with its emphasis on waveforms, energy forces and matter particles came to mind. So did the concept of a global involvement. I was determined to expand the investigation, to get past the reliance on yin-yang and a Mobius strip. The problem was growing, but becoming more focused; my thinking began to run more broadly across several concepts, yet more deeply, too.

Stages of the Design Process

A GOOD MARK should seem inevitable, as effortless as a Willie Mays catch, as classic as Bogart. The mark should seem, on first viewing, to have always been present, to have been placed on earth along with the rocks and trees and clouds. Despite appearances, this peculiar ring of timeless familiarity is not achieved easily.

While this book concentrates on the developmental planning of a mark, planning is only the beginning of the entire life of a mark. It is important to show how planning relates to the later stages of the graphic design process.

The process consists of seven stages, illustrated in the accompanying diagram.

Defining the Problem

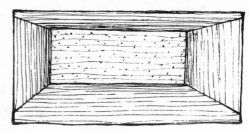

Before you begin firing off concept sketches, you have to know where you are headed. It is very important to define the problem and the goals that you and the client are setting. Walking into the first meeting with a client is a lot like walking into a white room with no windows or doors. At that moment you have no sense of what the goal will be, much less a notion of how to get there. During the client briefing, your job is to gain

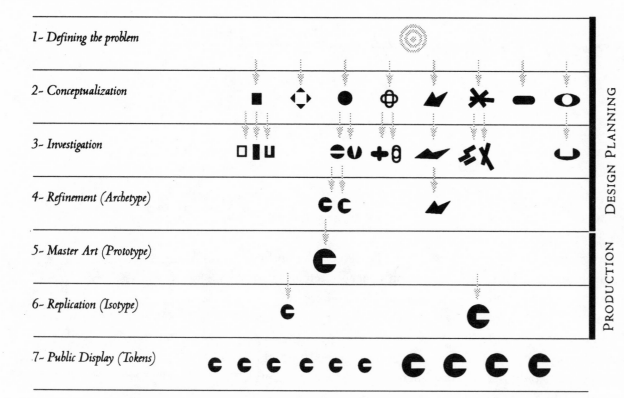

1- *Defining the problem*

2- *Conceptualization*

3- *Investigation*

4- *Refinement (Archetype)*

5- *Master Art (Prototype)*

6- *Replication (Isotype)*

7- *Public Display (Tokens)*

DESIGN PLANNING

PRODUCTION

Defining the problem and articulating the goals may take several meetings and involve extensive research. Time spent on this process is time well spent, because the last thing you want to do is start off on your journey with only a hazy sense of where you are headed. All the analysis that you will be doing in the succeeding phases will be based on what you have learned from this stage. Give your client plenty of feedback to be sure that you both see the problem the same way, setting the same goal. When you think that you understand as complete an understanding of the problem as possible. You, in that white featureless room, are receiving a description of a far-off place that is your goal. You are about to attempt to travel to that place, but first you must gather as much information as possible to guide your journey.

the matter, write a summary, known as a *project overview* or *brief*, and send a copy to the client.

You are still in a featureless white room, but you have an excellent description of your destination.

Conceptualization

It is time to create some openings in your white room that will permit you to see into the surrounding countryside. Each concept is a door in the wall. The more doors you can create, the better will be your odds of finding a suitable path leading to your destination. At this point, you will want to be fairly irrational, trying to pour out as many ideas as possible whether you think they are likely to be helpful or not. Just create as many doors as you can. Create so many doors that you eliminate the wall. Later you can use some judgment about which doors to go through—which sketches to explore.

The process of conceptualization is sometimes called thumbnail sketching because it is common to make small, very rough drawings about the size of your thumb-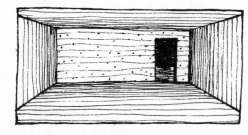nail. In fact, any material, technique or size can be used to generate ideas; what does seem to be important for most designers is that the conceptual sketches be rough. Too much concern for precision at this stage will draw you out through the door and too far down the path that may turn out to be leading in the wrong direction. Worse, it may blind you to related ideas. Looking at a rough drawing suggests, by its ambiguity, two or three alternatives. Viewing a precise drawing suggests only itself. Even using a computer, which makes precision almost effortless, is a dangerous practice simply because the output is too defined.

Conceptualizing is a process of jotting, of allowing hazy, indistinct marks to trigger more ideas and begin a feedback loop. You want to get everything out—the good, the bad and the ugly. You want to keep the flow of new ideas going as long as possible. Stop when the well is dry or when the work becomes tedious. Begin again when you are fresh and relaxed.

Remember that concepts rarely arrive fully formed—the sketches do not record your pre-existing ideas. Rather, it is by sketching that you allow ideas to be worked out. Ideas are a kind of motivation; the sketching itself is the creation.

The misconception that one gets an idea and then puts it down on paper impedes creation. Many students hesitate to begin. They are waiting for an idea, as if the idea will be fully presented in their mind's eye. They think that if they can just spend a little more time envisioning the idea, they will capture it as film captures a scene. Of course, the idea never quite arrives in detailed form. Fuzzy and indistinct, it slips away just at the moment of putting it down. The sketch never looks like the idea; it even seems to chase the idea away.

How do you start the feedback loop? Do what kids in a sandbox do—play with the medium. Kids will run their hands through the sand, pick up a glob and squeeze it, taste it, pour it. They don't get into the sandbox with blueprints for a sandcastle. The structures evolve from sensing the interaction of the material. Doodle. Scribble. Make shapes and marks of anything at all. Sketch anything that comes into your mind. Look at the sketches carefully. More ideas will come from them. This playful cycle is the core of the conceptualizing process and the heart of designing.

Investigation

The next stage is to select some of the conceptual sketches for further treatment. Investigate them to see what potential they have. You are stepping through the doors (conceptual sketches), looking around and, based on your knowledge of the goal, selecting the doors that offer the promise of a quick path to the promised land.

Investigative sketches examine modifications of the chosen thumbnails. Sometimes the conceptual sketches are combined. Tracing paper or computers are often used to retain a given feature while other features are altered. In this way, a chosen conceptual sketch branches into several related concepts, each of which may contain several iterations.

Investigation is an analytical phase. You need to be aware of the goal so that you do not waste time on sketches that, no matter how intrinsically interesting, lead you astray. This is a time of making hard choices. The playfulness that in conceptualizing was almost random is replaced by a more directed and reasoned process.

Yet play is not eliminated. The modification of selected conceptual sketches still needs looseness and experimentation. Try to think of every possible way a given sketch could be transformed. Call on tried-and-true manipulative techniques: cutting, patterning, changing from line to solid, figure and ground ambiguities, repeating—any kind of technique that can change the visual form of the initial sketch.

Through the investigations, you will conclude that one or two of the basic concepts have

more promise than the others. When you are certain that you have explored the ideas sufficiently to decide which ones are best, it is time to refine them.

Refinement

Refinement takes a great deal of time. You are fairly sure you have a concept that will solve the problem. Now your job is to polish it. Final decisions about the way the mark should look are made at this stage. This is a good time to work on the computer or with mechanical drafting tools on responsive materials.

What are the exact proportions for the mark? Nail down the precise dimensions of each element and the relationships of each of the elements to one another. The mark must be fleshed out now and fully composed. Optical illusions that may be distracting must be resolved, interesting ones enhanced.

If conceptual sketches are analogous to placing doors in the featureless room and investigation is taking the first steps out those doors to explore where the paths lead, then refinement is following the trail all the way to the goal. It is the process that leads you right up to the solution. Analysis has a greater role than play, although there is still a tremendous need to be sensitive to the nuances of the iterations. Each decision is carefully evaluated for likely problems that might occur when the logo is in use.

The result of the refinement stage is called the *archetype*. The archetype is not a drawing, but it is the evident idea that is represented by the most fully developed refined sketch. It is a clearly manifested ideal that guides the execution of the master artwork. The refined sketch may be imperfect in its execution; still, it is very explicit in pointing to the archetype.

Master Art

Refinement leads you to the solution; it reveals the archetype. Now the goal is to approximate the archetype as closely as possible in physical form. The master drawing is an attempt to embody the archetype, to give it flesh and blood. The archetype is an ideal—no physical construct can be a perfect realization. Nevertheless, you need to take the rather presumptuous view that your piece of master art will somehow be able to transcend this rule and be perfect in every respect. Play and analysis are both submerged, the master drawing is an exercise in technique. It is not necessary that the designer be the drafter of the master artwork (although this is often the case). What is required in any event is total control and understanding of the tools and means of production so that the drawing is fine.

Drawing the master art results in the *prototype.* It is the original physical mark, the parent from which all realized versions will descend.

Traditionally, the prototype existed as a pen and ink (or ambercell) drawing stored in someone's flat file. Today the prototype commonly exists as computer information, stored in copyable disks. Either way, it is vital that the prototype be clearly labeled and permanently stored.

Replication

Reproductions made directly from the prototype are known as *isotypes* (*iso* means alike or identical). These may be photostats or computer-encoded format. Isotypes become the direct artwork for all of the uses of the mark.

Isotypes are one generation removed from the prototype, and no replicated mark originating from the host should be made from anything other than an isotype. This dictum does not cover electrostatic copies, faxes or other reproductions, however. The degradation that occurs with fax, electrostatic copies, and other reproductions makes it all the more important that the isotype be faithfully used for replication.

Public Display

Each version of the mark in its reproduced form in public display is known as a *token*. The tokens are the individual samples of the mark in use. They are the foot soldiers in the campaign to identify the host. The ultimate effort in any visual identification project is to control the manner in which tokens are perceived. The critical issue in mastering, replicating and displaying the mark is to ensure that in the process of moving from single prototype to the many tokens seen by the public, there be as close an approximation of the archetype as possible.

The steps of defining the problem and the conceptualization, investigation and refinement of the solution yielding the archetype are *planning* functions. Making and replicating the master art, including printing, are *production* functions. Graphic designers are generally involved in the first stage, defining the problem, although occasionally this vital work is ceded to account representatives. The next three stages are the heart of the graphic designer's profession. Usually the designer also produces the prototype, although relinquishing this production task is not a problem as long as the production artist is skilled and the refined sketches clearly articulate the archetype. Graphic designers are occasionally involved in other replication and production tasks, although these are further removed from the essential core of design.

Sketch 078(5.1)

Sketch 079(6.1)

Sketch 080(7.1)

Sketch 081(8.1)

For the next series of sketches, the problem becomes how to design an emblem that can stand in as an 'O' in the logotype while expressing the concept of technology and biomedical research. While traces of yin-yang remain in these sketches, the intention is to take a fresh approach to the problem. The first three sketches—78, 79, 80—are attempts to imagine a line or shape animated, moving through space or time. This leads naturally to designs that introduce rhythmic elements, such as the parallel grid that appears in sketch 81.

The next sketch, 82, introduces a waveform that, while reminiscent of the yin-yang, adopts a more flattened sine wave aspect. Sketch 84, a look at what an endless strand (Mobius strip, DNA?) might look like under a microscope, is immediately shelved and the sine waves reappear in sketch 85.

Sketches 85 and 86 are pivotal sketches at this stage. They combine elements of three key themes: the waveforms suggest the yin-yang, elemental physical forces and movement. Conceptually, the idea reflects a blending of Asian philosophy and Western physics and a compatibility with biological processes such as growth and exchange.

Sketch 086(12.2)

Sketch 087(12.3)

Sketch 088(12.4)

The references are far too subtle for a viewer to be consciously aware of these relationships, yet the idea could be successful even if the connection is subliminal. What is vitally important is that the symbol, regardless of abstractions, be visually exciting and compelling. The first three lines of sketch 80 have been resurrected here. Instead of continuing the sequence into an infinity sign, the sequence regresses into a straight line. The repetition of the positive and negative wave cycles creates a pattern that catches the eye. There is change, yet stability. The mark strikes an attitude as it holds attention, becomes memorable. It is becoming visually exciting.

The new sketches are immediately inserted into the logotype to test the visibility and size relationships (sketches 87, 88).

41

The hint of three-dimensionality in these latest marks triggers a new idea. Perhaps a sphere (representing the globe?) could be manipulated in a similar way. The next 13 sketches (89–101) investigate some possibilities along this line. Waveforms and Mobius strips are introduced into the sphere.

Sketch 097(13.9)

Sketch 098(14.1)

Sketch 099(14.2)

Sketch 100(14.3)

Sketch 101(14.4)

Sketch 102(12.5)

Sketch103(12.6)

Sketch 104(12.7)

Sketch 105(12.85)

*Sketches 102–106: Problems persist. The
spheres are resistant to clear reading or seem too
complex. Attention returns to the oscillating
waveforms. They are drawn more carefully, then are
tried in both positive and negative formats.*

In sketch 106, *a surprising trait is noticed. When the waveforms come together, they create two bright "nodes," or spots. The nodes create a diagonal vector (line of force or flow of attention) reinforcing the slope of the waveform. This optical illusion is a positive development, since the nodes create another level of interest in the mark. They also aid the conceptual foundation of the mark: a visualization of the concept from physics that particles of matter are bundles of energy forces.*

Sketch 107(12.10)   *Sketch108(12.11)*   *Sketch 109(12.12)*

BI S

Typography is further investigated in the next three sketches. The symbol that emerges is somewhat complex. The typography will need to be simple, elegant, perhaps somewhat primal. One thinks of Greek lapidary inscriptions. Can the 'S' reflect the sine waveform shape?

Sketch 110(12.13)

Sketch 111(12.14)

Sketch 112(12.15)

Sketch 113(12.16)

Sketches 110–117: It is time to put the sketches into a format that can be shown to Will. I will show him many of the sketches that I have done, even though they are in very rough form. But the principal candidates, which are the culmination of a series of discoveries within each line of thought, need to be sketched more carefully and presented in a larger size. Thinking about details is more important now. The logo shifts from investigative inquiries to refinements.

Sketches 110, 111 and 112 are modules from which versions of the mark can be traced. The mark's appearance is greatly changed by small differences in the weight of the lines, the distance between lines and the number of the lines in the pattern. These first two modules give me extremely different structures from which to work.

(For this kind of drawing, it may be worthwhile to use a computer drawing program. Others find that the hand and eye are precise and quick enough for what is needed at this stage and that these kinds of development sketches are aided by the touch of the human hand, not the click of the mouse. The important thing is that the designer be focused on the visual

nature of the mark, not the implementation of technique.)

Sketch 115: The lines are much more distinctive when they are reversed out than when they appear as black lines on a white background. In this version the distinct nodes are lost, in part because the lines don't touch, and in part because of the positioning of two of the convergences at the perimeter of the disk.

Sketches 118–125: Large-scale interpretations of the wave-particle logotype are prepared. The investigation of the typeface continues with the proportion of the emblem held fairly constant. The version based on the typeface Bodoni (sketch 124) has a remarkable clarity and harmony between the weight of the thicks and thins within the typeface and the weights within the emblem. It also connotes rationality and the

enlightenment. The ability of the weight of the serifs to match the diacritical mark over the emblem is noted.

Sketches 126–134: Even though I expect to carry a thick sheaf of papers into the discussion with Will, a few remaining ideas want to trickle forth. These sketches show three different directions, although each was triggered by ideas already explored.

Sketch 126 is overlapping of the spheroid in sketch 91. It conjures atomic forces in a very 1950s way, which is also the cause for its abandonment.

Sketches 127 and 128 look at waveforms that are slightly out of phase, which creates an interesting visual effect. The appearance of the somewhat calligraphic strokes suggests filling in the spaces to create broader waves.

The broad waves are investigated in sketches 129, 130 and 131. These are also appealing, but at this point the line of thought is interrupted—perhaps because it is not clear where the idea should go.

A different direction is taken with 132. Imagine three pebbles hitting the surface of a calm pond simultaneously. The ripple waves interfere with one another and make a very interesting pattern. This idea is hurriedly sketched as a logotype in both positive and negative format. This idea was sketched the morning of my presentation.

I collect my sketches, select and arrange the major lines of thinking, and go off to my meeting with Will LaValley. It is 3:00 in the afternoon, two weeks after our initial conversation.

III. Details
Perils of the Creative Process

*U*NLIKE THE occasion of my first presentation to Will, this time I felt a little apprehensive. I carried an idea that I thought was especially interesting, and I wanted him to be excited about it, too. As before, I sequenced the drawings in chronological order, showing each concept's development and talking about the strengths and weaknesses of each.

The agreement to work on an emblem to be placed into the logotype in place of the 'O' allowed me to concentrate solely on round forms. The real issue was which metaphor for BIOS seemed most appropriate and which emblem seemed to capture the spirit of the enterprise most effectively.

I hoped that Will would be struck by the optical illusion of the waves and nodes. It was obvious that most of my sketches were working out visual details of that concept, so when I offered what I thought was the most effective mark, it came as no surprise to him. He was already comparing the different line weights and talking about how color could be applied. He grasped the connection of waveforms and particles at once, although I assured him that the effectiveness of the emblem did not rest on the viewer having an interest in subatomic particle physics.

After only 45 minutes, the issue seemed settled. I would proceed with the next stage, refining the mark in every detail. I was anxious to begin and pleased that Will was satisfied.

Perils of the Creative Process

CLIENTS AND designers are both in rather insecure positions when they come together. The client depends on the designer's experience, creativity and judgment in creating the visible face that the host presents to the public. The designer needs the client's approval before any work can become realized. The economic structure is a source of tension, too: The designer needs a satisfied client to continue paying the bills; the client pays out a good sum with only the hope and trust that the results will be acceptable.

This tender interaction of designer and client is not helped by the ambiguous position that the graphic design profession occupies. Terms such as "graphic artist" and "commercial artist" still abound, and when practitioners accept these terms on equal footing to the term "designer," a blurring of the planning (creative analysis) and production (technical) roles is inevitable. From the designer's perspective, three misconceptions arise particularly frequently.

I Need a Pair of Hands

When Will LaValley initially called me, he mentioned that he had an idea in mind and simply needed someone to "draw it up" for him. This is a classic statement of the "I Need a Pair of Hands" syndrome. The designer is placed in an awkward situation because the client is revealing that he doesn't understand the design process. The client is looking for a production artist, not a planner. In some cases, the client's misunderstanding of the process runs so deeply that the designer must refuse the project and refer the client to a printer or someone involved in production. Politely educate the client about the planning aspects of graphic design so that some other designer will not have to go through this painful experience. Then go out for a beer; you've just realized once again that most people haven't the slightest idea of what designers do.

The Fishing Trip

A second type of client/designer problem that impedes creative solutions is the fishing trip. With the fishing trip, the client at least has an understanding that the creative input of the designer is necessary. The difficulty is that the client and the designer have done a poor job of pinpointing the problem to be solved. Unlike sport fishing, logo fishing can be a very stressful type of behavior for everyone involved.

During a fishing trip, the designer is used as a kind of rod and reel. Cast for a logo, reel it in, take a look. The client examines the logo with great interest and then asks for another try. After all, what's the chance that the biggest and best fish has been caught with the first cast? The designer casts again, reels in another logo, the client expresses some interest but not total approval. Try again, "I'll know it when I see it" (which really means "after I've compared enough samples").

It doesn't require many casts before the designer is reduced to a random event generator, hoping that something might please the client but having no sense of what that may be. The client may not have a notion either, but like any angler feels sure that the big one is bound to be reeled in on the next line. While fishing, the client and the designer cease to think about the process of problem solving. Before long, the client is just curious what the next catch will be, and the designer is simply anxious for something—anything—to satisfy the client. Before long, both are frustrated.

Two policies can alleviate fishing trip tendencies. First, be sure the client's problem has been clearly defined and the goal articulated. Then, be sure that the logo is targeted to solve the problem, not please the client. This puts the emphasis on analysis and meeting objectives. When the target is focused, you avoid the murky waters

of the fishing trip. Both the client and the designer can see when the target is struck. Of course, there's always the nagging possibility that some other design could come closer to the bull's-eye. This is why the second policy is so important.

The second policy is to be sure that clients pay for revisions and redesigns. The first designs may look a lot better to your clients if they know they have to pay for second or third attempts. If you are working in good faith with your clients and you give your work your best effort, this procedure will generally lead to a satisfactory solution. If you and your clients should seriously disagree about the solution, you can sit down and renegotiate the aims and objectives. Of course, this may result in a decision to part ways, but that is a more professional, and in the end more satisfying, course of action than endless fishing.

The Shirt Sale

In the shirt sale, the designer is encouraged to present several ideas to give the client a selection. If a client says, "I like to make choices from a menu of possibilities," you can expect a shirt sale problem. The client wants you to present three, four, five or more designs from which the winner will be chosen. You just line up the shirts and the client will pick the one that suits him best.

So what's the difficulty with the shirt sale scheme? First, assuming the problem has been well researched and clearly defined, it is unlikely that three designs will each be equally effective at solving the problem. It's the designer's responsibility to investigate the problem and the potential solutions so thoroughly that the best solution is isolated. To show a client solutions that you know are inferior is unrewarding and unethical.

Second, it is an inefficient use of your time and your client's money. The development and refinement of three or four solutions takes three or four times as long. The cost is tripled or quadrupled or, as more often is the case, you end up spending only one-third as much time as you should on each solution to make the project affordable to the client. It's no surprise that when the time comes to present, you walk into the boardroom carrying three weak solutions. You

59

aren't proud of them, you don't believe in them and, as a result, all you can do is offer them and hope for the best.

In this situation, what is the best outcome? The board may approve one of your decisions, and then you are sentenced to apply that weak mark to every piece of property the company owns. You are not likely to feel very good about that.

The outcome probably will not be that rosy. A client asks for a shirt sale approach because of the mistaken premise that it is easier to choose from three designs than from one. If you are presenting to a board of directors, for example, chances are that two board members will like version A, two version B, and two will hold out for version C. Then you will certainly be asked to combine them all into one logo. Now you have the unpleasant task of taking features from three weak marks and putting them together. The whole will be a great deal less than the sum of the parts.

Healthier Procedures

STRUCTURING THE discussions with clients can lead to happier outcomes for all involved. Select from two alternatives.

The Phased Approach

In the phased approach, the work is divided into chunks, called phases, and the designer presents the best solution for the work at each phase. The client pays the designer a fee to begin work, another installment upon presentation of the work and a final installment upon completion. The designer usually agrees to make small revisions after the presentation at no extra charge, to take into account any problems that might have been identified at that stage.

The phased approach is the standard industry practice. It allows the designer to become fully engaged on the task and emphasizes analysis and solving of the problem, yet allows the client to respond to the work at designated checkpoints.

The Open-Book Alternative

The BIOS project developed a little differently. We agreed that a fee would be based on very small steps of the process. I showed him virtually all the directions my thinking traveled, in very rough form, and we discussed the merits of each direction. Either of us could cancel the project at any time. As Will saw the process of my thinking and as the project developed further, his responses grew more helpful. He responded to the overall psychological feeling the mark elicited, avoiding the temptation to suggest specific visual features. I became more aware of the nature of the BIOS Foundation and sensitive to the kind of emotional posture the mark would have to assume.

Most clients would not have had an interest in such minutiae of the design process, but Will was quite eager to see it all. I would not have continued this method of design development if I had found that we were at loggerheads at each meeting; but in this case we enjoyed a mutual respect, agreed-upon goals and beneficial discussion of alternatives. My work became an open book for both of us to analyze and critique.

With an open book process, there is no formality to the final presentation because there are no surprises. The client is kept informed about movement toward the target as it unfolds. Because it was a small project involving only one person as the client, I did not have to worry about conflicting personalities. The technique was unconventional, but gratifying.

Self-Imposed Blocks to Creativity

YOUR RELATIONSHIP with the client can retard creative problem solving; but sometimes designers are their own worst enemies. The way you approach a problem and how you grapple with it can restrict your creative vision. Here are some methods of working that tend to thwart creative ideas.

The Mozart Approach

In the movie *Amadeus*, an opera impresario calls on Mozart to ask how the work is progressing on the score he commissioned. After all, rehearsals need to begin soon. The opera is finished, Mozart replies. Great, where is it? urges the excited theater mogul. Mozart simply smiles and taps his head. The opera is complete, he tells the impresario. All that remains is to put it down on paper.

Some designers take a Mozart approach. They believe they can plan the whole design in their minds and then simply transcribe it to paper. Mozart may have been able to compose entire operas in his head, but those of us who are not geniuses generally work in the opposite direction. The ideas come to us from looking at concrete things. The way to generate ideas is by looking at previous ideas. Even doodling will generate a feedback response that will lead somewhere. Then you can evaluate whether that somewhere is a positive or negative direction. Instead of staring at a blank sheet of paper, begin working.

The Beeline

In the beeline approach, the first interesting idea is rushed to completion. The beeline is an insufficient investigation of possibilities or a constriction of ideas because not enough time is spent generating concepts. Designers may become infatuated with the first decent thumbnail, immediately refine it and offer it as a solution. While this approach saves time, it rarely yields the best solutions. Each thumbnail sketch is a possible path. Some of these paths will be more promising than others. How do you know that your first idea is the best until you have given some thought to others? Spend enough time exploring possibilities so that by the time you move to other stages of the design

process you can be fairly certain that you have covered a lot of directions.

Your use of materials can help you get new ideas. I once assisted a designer in Atlanta on a project designing a series of symbols for IBM. I had a lot of respect for this designer and for the design team at IBM, so I pulled out all the stops. My ideas were well received, but the designer later admonished me about my design process.

"When working on your sketches, you don't try enough materials," he began. "In each of those sketches, you used a marker and tracing paper. The material you use affects your ability to generate ideas. If you were to use different materials, you would come up with more ideas." He explained that he made a practice of working with modeling clay for every problem he worked on. I have always thought that this was wise advice. Thumbnails can be cut paper, brushed paint, chalked and even modeled in clay as well as drawn with pencil or marker.

The beeline approach also closes off inspiration from other areas. In graduate school, I studied with a Korean sculptor and packaging designer named John Pai. One of the most inspirational teachers I have known, Pai assigned us one week to solve a consumer packaging problem by borrowing an idea from nature. We were to submit a drawing of the natural object—one that would also explain how it worked. Then we were to prepare a model of the consumer package based on nature's concept. The results were astounding.

"Every idea that you can ever think of," I remember him saying, "has already been employed in the natural world. All you have to do is observe." Allowing yourself to meander into other worlds leaves yourself open to new and creative solutions to problems.

The Template

More than one million years ago a primate known as *homo erectus* was busily surviving with the aid of the first stone tools. One of these tools was a teardrop-shaped implement with sharp cutting edges known as a handaxe. The handaxe became one of the longest surviving products of industry, outliving the era of *homo erectus* and continuing

virtually unchanged into the time of our own species. To realize the success of this stone implement, consider that the wheel is less than 10,000 years old; the handaxe lasted more than 100 times longer. Throughout its era, the handaxe was always made to fit a certain proportion. Whether the axe was large or small, the relationship of length to width was invariably 1.6 to 1.

This is curious. Wheels are always a certain proportion too, but wheels must be circular so they can roll—it is not so obvious that handaxes could function only when they fit a particular proportion. It is as if the people who made handaxes carried around in their memories a kind of template for handaxes. The template could be scaled to any size, but for it to be called a handaxe, it had to be the particular proportion that conformed to the template. Such a template may have proven useful in a prelingual or prehistoric society. Information could be passed on in a regimented, unvarying manner. A handaxe by definition was a tool of certain features and proportions; a grinder, a tool of different features and proportions. The proportion was one of the chacteristics of handaxeness. In this way, tools stayed in tightly controlled categories, while techniques for making them were passed along from generation to generation. A stone age designer did not have to stop and think how an axe should look or how it should be made. Since the only variable was size, the stone age designer could simply set about making it.

What the mental template inhibited was a response to new problems. As *homo sapiens* settled in larger social clusters and lived in villages where structures needed to be sturdy and permanent, survival presented a different set of problems. New social patterns required a greater variety of tools, tools specifically designed to accomplish tasks that were different from cutting and scraping. Archeologists identify these early village sites by the abundance and diversity of the tools found there. The sudden shift to diverse tools, to ingenious solutions to new problems, has caused archeologists to identify members of this class as a separate subspecies—*homo sapiens sapiens. Sapiens sapiens*

seemed to treasure creativity from the start. As every living human is a member of that subspecies, it is no wonder that every culture values creativity.

The ability to find new ways to solve problems is at the core of our being, but the template of our older, single-*sapiens*-selves is still present, too. If a designer in the United States is asked to design a letterhead, the thumbnail sketches will usually involve drawings in rectangular spaces with a 1.3 to 1 proportion, that of an 8.5" × 11" piece of paper. The designer may have some valid economic reasons to select a page of that size, but part of the reason is that the conventional usage of the word "letterhead" suggests a particular proportion, which is adopted without question. The template of "letterhead" is a 1.3 to 1 vertical sheet of paper. If you unconsciously accept the template, you miss the opportunity to use the paper horizontally, or to use a square sheet of paper, or to use mylar instead of paper.

Unacknowledged, templates stay in the subconscious, governing decisions in ways that retard creativity. If the designer can be aware of templating, each conventional template can be challenged, adopted or rejected as the problem at hand requires.

Distractions

When you work on a problem, allow that problem to be always present in your mind, either consciously when you focus on it, or unconsciously at other times. Many things will distract you from your goal. Some of these distractions may fool you into thinking that they are not distractions at all.

For instance, you may worry about the time and expense of the project. Think about those concerns before you begin designing—while you are working up the estimate and the contract. Once designing is under way, you must allow the creative process to dominate your thoughts totally. If you worry that you are spending too much time, you will fail to explore the problem fully. Perhaps you failed to appreciate how long the process would take or how much it would cost. You can pause and try to renegotiate the contract, but if you are in a design planning mode, you must not interfere with the free flow of concepts. Your responsibility now is to grapple with your ideas and creative solutions and meet the project's requirements. Concern about time and money must be excluded from the creative phase.

Perhaps you find that you are worrying about the client's tastes. Will she like this one or that one? He likes to wear blue, maybe I should refine the blue version. It is tempting to engage in this kind of daydream, but you must always keep in mind that the client will be best served and most content when the problem itself is solved. The problem is a third entity that is removed from your or your client's subjective preferences. If you have done a good job isolating the problem, then you will solve it. If you solve the problem, the client will be pleased.

It is time to refine the concept further. How many lines are required? What should their weights be? Should they overlap at the intersections, or just touch? What should be the precise shape of the waves? Sketches 135 and 136 begin that exploration.

Four variables must be investigated: the distance from crest to trough (frequency), the height of the crest (amplitude), the weight of the line, and the amount of overlap when lines touch. To help clarify these issues, I made skeletal waves called armatures. I could then build up the weight of the lines in a consistent fashion, keeping the basic flow of the waves constant.

Sketch 137(12.D22)

Sketch 138(12.D23)

Sketch 139(12.D25)

Sketch 140(12.D21)

Sketches 137–140 showed me immediately that the weight of the line was critical. Sketch 140 completely loses the flow of the lines, becoming instead black crescents on a white ground. Since part of the concept involved the illusion of two particles where the waveforms overlap, the weight and spacing had to be carefully worked out. Changing one element often had unforeseen consequences on others.

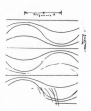

Soon two basic armatures evolved. Sketch 141 shows armature A with a frequency of one (a sine wave with a frequency equal to the diameter of the disk). For waves of large amplitude, such as shown in sketch 143, this has the effect of placing the nodes (the spots where the waves overlap) well within the confines of the perimeter of the mark. Waves with smaller amplitudes (sketch 144) or thinner lines (as in sketches 145 and 146) begin to create additional nodes. This is particularly distracting in sketch 144, where the thick lines become background and "beach balls" begin to emerge.

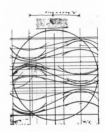

Armature B (sketch 147) takes a different approach. Although the frequency is still equal to the diameter of the circle, it is not a true sine wave. The outer portions of the wave are more steep, the central portion is stretched. Sketches based on armature B tend to have the nodes positioned close to the edges of the disk. I thought this might create an interesting tension or illusion between "outside" and "inside." Instead, it simply caused problems with very small fragments of black space, which would surely be lost in small sizes. To my eye, sketch 142 most clearly expressed the nodes in a comfortable yet active way.

73

Sketch 149(12.G20)

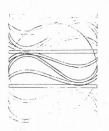

Sketch 150(12.G21)

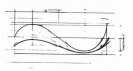

Sketch 151(12.G22)

Sketch 152(12.H20)

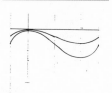

Sketch 153(12.H21)

Sketch 154(12.H22)

Sketch 155(12.H23)

IV. Fresh Ideas
Categories of Marks

THE CLIENT always needs a period of time to become familiar with a new design. Just as the designer hangs sketches in the work environment to live with the design, so the client must spend some time with the proposed mark.

Even though Will LaValley seemed pleased with the direction of the BIOS logo, something was making him uncomfortable. The nature of this became clear after my second presentation.

"Steve, I've been thinking about the mark and I think there are some problems, minor I'm sure, but they need to be addressed. At the meeting today, I wasn't sure how to express the feeling I want to achieve, or what I find wanting in the proposed logo. This logo needs to have more vibration and excitement. It needs more energy. This mark feels flat, both in terms of being two-dimensional but also in terms of emotion. The lines, while interesting, are not exciting enough. Can't something be done to impart more feeling, more excitement?"

The conversation lasted for almost an hour. It was, of course, disappointing to discover that Will wasn't as excited about the mark as I was. Designers always feel the need to retain the present iteration of a mark, the client has a natural resistance to accepting it because being something new, it involves change. I needed to determine if Will's comments stemmed from a sincere analysis of the expressive needs of the mark, or if he was embarking on a fishing trip.

"Will, can you be more specific about what it is that disturbs you?"

"Well, I can't say exactly what is wrong or what to do to fix it, all I know is that I think it is important that this mark be very active and kinetic. Right now, it's just a bit too static. I tried during our meeting to visualize movement in it, but the more I looked at those lines this evening, the more they seem to me to be fixed in place."

I hesitated to disagree with him, suppressing the natural desire to defend the result of my efforts. I needed to sound him out, to understand his viewpoint. There was a moment of silence as I tried to think of something to say.

Finally, "I cannot say whether this is the best of all possible marks for BIOS. I can say that it is the best I could do in the time provided to this point. Furthermore, I believe it is a strong emblem that resonates with your needs . . ."

"That's it, that's just the word, Steve," Will interrupted. "Resonance. It needs to resonate within the emblem. If it can resonate, it will be more active, plus it will relate to the kind of research we want to sponsor. It suggests the resonance of differing cultures. Can't you make it resonate a little more?"

"Will, I'll tell you what I'm concerned about. It's possible that I can go back and look at it some more but will you know when it's resonating enough? This is all a relative business here, and it's so slippery. Suppose I work for another two weeks and you are still unsure? What do you do then, go out and get another designer and begin from scratch?"

"I would hope not. I like the way we're working."

"Well, Will, it's certainly your prerogative to do just that, but what I'm trying to ensure is that you don't get into a quagmire, constantly wondering if a better solution might be out there."

He paused before speaking. "Steve, I respect your work here and I don't dislike the mark at the place it is now. But I have to tell you that I think you can discover a way of injecting more movement, more vibration, more resonance into the emblem. When you do that, I will have something that I can proudly display for the foundation and you will have something that you can be proud of, too."

I was satisfied that Will was honestly and clearly articulating a direction that the mark needed to convey. Will was not fishing; on the contrary, it was I who had not fished deeply enough in defining the problem. I had failed to realize the importance of an active mark. After our conversation, I felt the problem had been redefined in a concrete way. I agreed to start over.

Categories of Marks

*F*OUR BASIC types of marks function as logos. Each has its own set of advantages and limitations.

Pictographs

Pictographs are pictures that have been reduced to essentials. Predating written language, they can be found in early cave paintings and Native American petroglyphs. Pictographs have some very clear advantages as logos. Because they are very simple yet depict the essential traits of objects, they are very effective as symbols. They do not depend on language or literacy to get their message across. Because they communicate efficiently, requiring very little visual detail, they are versatile in the ways they can be reproduced and displayed. They can be reduced to very small sizes and applied to virtually any material.

The liability in using a pictograph is that it may prove too limited as a symbol of the host. For instance, if the host is a company that makes only toy apples, then perhaps a pictographic apple would be a fine choice, but if the company expands its line to include toy cars, then the pictographic mark may suddenly prove insufficient. Pictographs are difficult to use when there is no simple object or product to picture. If an insurance company needs a mark, it is difficult to use a pictograph of their product.

In some cases an object that symbolizes a characteristic of the host can be adopted. Then it is possible to design a pictograph of that object as a metaphor. For instance, Traveler's Insurance Co. uses an umbrella as a symbol of protection. A commonly understood symbol is adopted for a host whose activities cannot be easily visualized. Pictographs of such symbols are obvious solutions. Still, in some cases, the meaning of the symbol may have to be taught to the public and the connection of the symbol to the host must be reinforced.

Ideographs

Ideographs are abstract designs that do not represent real objects but instead are interesting geometric devices in and of themselves. Ideographs have the advantage of being related solely to the host. Whereas an umbrella may contain many associations in addition to Traveler's Insurance Co., an ideograph such as the Chase Manhattan mark relates directly to the bank. Ideographs share with pictographs the advantage of being free of the restrictions of language, working well in multilingual environments.

The disadvantage of ideographs is that because the mark is abstract, the mark has no clear relationship to the host. The public must learn the mark, requiring the public to be educated by repeated and frequent displays. Because of this need for a heavy dose of education, ideographs are usually suited to hosts that enjoy a great deal of print and media exposure.

Logotypes

In the days when printing was done from hot metal, a logotype was any frequently used word (such as "an" or "the") which was cast as one piece of type. Later, companies' emblems and names were cast as one-piece logotypes and used as signatures in ads. Today we use the word logotype to refer to a mark that employs the host's name spelled out.

Logotypes have the distinct advantage of being the only kind of mark that literally says the name of the company. It is the most direct form of mark in that it combines both visual and verbal information.

The colloquial name for the host is often more appropriate for adoption as the logotype than the full legal name. J. S. Campbell and Son, Inc. may be shortened to Campbell's. Test how the host answers the business phone. That name is usually the one that the host is known by to the public.

The advantages of a logotype are sometimes outweighed by its disadvantages. First there is the inevitable problem of being linguistically linked. Logotypes may lose their effectiveness in situations where another language is spoken. To a speaker of English, the word nova means star, but to a speaker of Spanish, "No va" means "It doesn't go." In a similar way, a host desiring to blend with a different culture may not want the aspect of difference to be emphasized by the foreignness of a word.

Besides the linguistic difficulties, the designer of a logotype is faced with another practical problem. If the word or words exceeds seven or eight characters in length, the mark tends to become complex, which restricts the amount of reduction the mark can withstand before it becomes illegible. It also means that if the characters are arranged horizontally, the proportion of length to height tends to become so great that the mark needs a lot of space to fit. These liabilities may not prove insurmountable, but remember that a mark should be versatile, giving the host as much freedom as possible in its application.

Monograms

The monogram walks the fine line between verbal and visual. Being an identifying mark combining one or more initial letters, the verbal short-hand of the monogram allows the visual form to be simpler than the logotype. By using a monogram, you avoid foreign words and literacy issues.

On the other hand, a monogram doesn't speak the name of the host unless the host uses the initials in daily activity. Columbia Broadcasting Service becomes CBS, International Business Machines becomes IBM, the Central Intelligence Agency becomes CIA. But Todd's TV Repair is unlikely to become known as TTVR. Citizen's Interstate Alliance cannot very well adopt it initials, nor would Beverly of Beverly's Salon wish to adopt initials. Remember, too, that a host's initial letters may also be the initial letters of several other concerns. Monograms are conveniences when a host has a very long name, but they do not say anything about the nature of the host's activities. The general rule of thumb is to avoid initial letters (monograms) unless two conditions are met: the host is already better known by the initials than by its full name, and the host has the resources to keep those initials in the public eye, thereby claiming that particular sequence of initials for itself.

Hybrid Forms

A LOGO CAN combine two or more of these types. Through the union of different types of marks, a logo may achieve the benefits of each. There are three pitfalls to avoid when combining categories of marks. Be aware that the mark will become more complex as more elements are added. Under those conditions, the first challenge is to maintain enough simplicity that the host can still use the logo effectively in a variety of sizes and materials. The second challenge is to control the design of the elements so that the overall mark has unity and looks like one mark instead of several unrelated parts. The third pitfall, one that is particularly crucial, is that you want the public to remember the logo as one central idea, not two or three. Double identification is the result of having two marks representing one host. It is as if the host had two faces or two names. Imagine how hard it would be to keep both of them straight and identify both names and faces with the same host. A logo must offer a single, clear face to the public. Only then will it be effectively remembered and recalled.

Sketch 156(18.1)

Sketch 157(19.1)

Sketch 158(20.1)

Sketch 159(20.2)

Sketch 160(20.3)

Sketch 161(21.1)

Sketch 162(22.1)

Sketch 163(22.2)

It is time to clear the memory banks and look at fresh alternatives. Each of the new sketches seeks to find a way of setting up more vibration, movement and energy. The idea of waves and particles is not forsaken. All the earlier ideas, even back to the yin-yang, are allowed to simmer in the background.

Beginning with sketch 158 and continuing through sketch 181, the attempt is to search for some kind of repeatable device or pattern that can provide a suitable vibration effect. Ideas of growth, numerical progressions and texture gradients are employed.

Sketch 164(22.3)

Sketch 165(23.1)

Sketch 166(24.1)

Sketch 167(24.A2)

Sketch 168(24.A3)

Sketch 169(24.B2)

Sketch 170(24.B3)

Sketch 171(24.B4)

Sketch 172(24.B5)

Sketch 173(24.B6)

Sketch 174(25.1)

Sketch 175(26.1)

Sketch 175 becomes a module. By repeating the module, a pattern is created. The module can be reversed, inverted and manipulated in a variety of ways.

Sketch 176(26.2)

Sketch 177(26.3)

Sketch 178(26.4)

Sketch 179(26.5)

The similar module in sketch 177 leads to some interesting studies in sketches 178–181. These sketches create an illusion of three dimensionality that is effective in holding interest and making the symbol active.

Sketch 180(26.6)

Sketch 181(26.7)

Sketch 182(27.1)

Sketch 183(28.1)

Sketch 184(28.2)

Sketch 185(28.3)

Sketch 186(28.4)

Sketch 187(28.5)

Sketches 183 and 184 suggest the idea of a ball or globe. This idea is explored more fully by adding the illusion of shading. The illusion of three dimensionality is quite compelling.

Sketch 188(28.6)

Sketch 189(28.7)

Sketch 190(28.8)

Sketch 191(28.9)

Sketch 192(28.10)

Sketch 193(28.11)

Sketch 194(28.12)

The logotype returns in sketch 189 as the ball is inserted into the word.

Sketches 190 through 194 look at the possibility of playing up the illusion of going from a flat surface to a sphere. The lines look flat until they wrap around the ball.

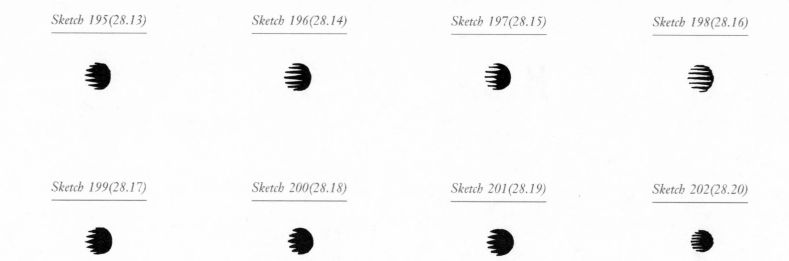

Sketch 195(28.13)

Sketch 196(28.14)

Sketch 197(28.15)

Sketch 198(28.16)

Sketch 199(28.17)

Sketch 200(28.18)

Sketch 201(28.19)

Sketch 202(28.20)

The next 10 sketches explore another way of shading the ball. The trick here is to create as much illusion of roundness as possible while using as few "teeth" as possible. It is necessary to look at the width of the shapes and how deeply the white teeth cut into the black circle.

Sketch 203(28.21)   *Sketch 204(28.22)*   *Sketch 205(28.23)*

Sketch 203 rather unexpectedly emerges.
Playing larger in sketch 205, it reintroduces the
yin-yang.

Sketch 206(29.1)

Sketch 207(29.2)

Sketch 208(29.3)

Sketch 209(29.4)

Sketch 210(30.1)

Sketch 211(30.2)

The idea of modulation is tried in sketches 206–210. Modulation involves a continuous change in some aspect of the mark. The change can be gradual (as in sketch 206) or abrupt (as in sketch 208).

Sketches 208 and 209 explore the idea of an indent, or depression, which attracts the eye in a way similar to the nodes.

Sketch 210 looks at what happens when a bar is slowly eclipsed by another shape such as a white disk. By sketch 213, this idea reaches a very rich stage in which the bar gets thinner before the negative area evolves into a black ellipse, which in turn grows thicker and straighter until it returns to the shape of the original bar.

Sketch 212(30.3)

Sketch 213(30.4)

Sketch 214(30.5)

Sketch 215(30.B6)

If sketch 213 is treated as a sort of supermodule, it can be arranged to form more complex, but orderly, compositions. Sketch 215 has the illusion of some fascinating chevron-shaped patterns within it.

Sketch 216(30.B7)   *Sketch 217(30.B8)*

Focusing on some of the activity within the supermodule, sketches 216 and 217 investigate the distinction between positive and negative forms.

Sketch 218(30.A6)

Sketch 219(30.A7)

Sketch 220(30.A8)

Sketch 221(30.B9)

Sketch 222(30.B10)

Sketch 223(30.B11)

After a blind alley (sketches 218, 219, 220), the supermodule is drawn larger (sketch 221). When paired with its inverted self (sketch 222), several unexpected arrow-like forms are created. While the arrows are not particularly helpful to the cause, the waveform that extends through the center is a happy accident (sketch 223).

Sketch 224(30.B12)	*Sketch 225(31.1)*	*Sketch 226(31.2)*	*Sketch 227(31.3)*

By cleaning up the symbol a bit, the arrows are eliminated and the waveform is enhanced (sketch 224).

Sketch 224 and the line of sketches preceding it are bilaterally symmetrical. The black and white areas are related but not identical forms. I decided to try to make a bilaterally symmetrical module in which the white areas are identical in form to the black areas. The module 225 can give that kind of effect.

Sketch 228(31.4)   *Sketch 229(31.5)*   *Sketch 230(31.6)*   *Sketch 231(31.7)*

The module is sketched carefully and then employed in several experiments. This module can produce the illusion of three dimensions. It can cause a surface to seem rounded or twisted. It vibrates and has a terrific amount of activity associated with it.

Sketch 229: A surface with a raised hump.
Sketch 230: Suggestive of a sphere, but ambiguous.
Sketch 231: Simpler pattern.

Sketch 232(31.8)   *Sketch 233(31.9)*   *Sketch 234(31.10)*   *Sketch 235(31.11)*

Sketch 232 creates a central "raised island" effect. It looks a bit like a trilobite. At this stage, even though not all of these forms relate specifically to the nature of BIOS, the effect of the vibration is interesting enough to warrant investigation on its own merits. So the sequence of sketches 227–240 is the result of playing with the module to see what it can do.

Sketches 233 and 234 represent attempts to reintroduce some content—in this case the yin-yang. But the effect of the yin-yang is not clear enough. Instead it looks like an 'S'.

With sketch 235 a final alteration is made to the basic module. Now it is regarded as something flexible along a horizontal axis. The waveform will span a distance governed by its location as a chord of

Sketch 236(31.B12)

Sketch 237(31.B13)

Sketch 238(31.A12)

Sketch 239(31.A13)

the disk. At the center, where the wave lies along the diameter of the disk, the waveform is long. But toward the top and bottom, the waves are shorter. This gives the interesting illusion of a flat surface around the rim and a bowl effect toward the center.

Sketches 236 and 237 are dead ends, neither enhancing nor extending the concept.

Sketch 238 is a simplified version of sketch 235.

Sketches 239 and 240 keep the length constant, varying instead the height (amplitude) of the waves.

Sketch 241 at first seems to come from nowhere, but it actually builds from sketch 235. It takes the central part of the bowl (i.e., without the rim) and simply inverts the bottom half. Surprisingly, the yin-yang comes back in a subtle way. This symbol plays tricks on the eye. It appears to rotate, it undulates in a push and pull motion, it has flowing, graceful lines to the waveforms.

In many ways this form resonates with the needs of BIOS. It fits the need to be very active, very vibrational. It is about waves and world (northern and southern hemispheres are suggested as well as east and west). Some problems still need to be addressed. How should the thin, outer edges be resolved? Sketch 242 investigates the outer edges as thin lines instead of recurring waves, but this mark lacks a sense of closure or completion. Sketch 243 looks at a six-step progression of waves, instead of four, while 244 is an attempt at a five-step progression.

102

V. Achieving Resonance
Functional Requirements of Marks

$\mathcal{F}$ROM THE moment he saw the first of the new sketches, Will was animated and enthusiastic. This time the initial conceptual sketches showed much greater variety and deeper investigation of possibilities. There was more "play" in the process and greater expression in the marks.

Will agreed immediately that series 31 was "it." I proposed that the emblem in sketch 241 be placed in the logotype with the typeface (Baskerville) used in sketch 194.

Back in the studio, I had much to do about refining the mark, making decisions about weight, number of lines and spacing between lines. It became clear that the lines should not extend past the emblem into the letters of the logotype (as they had in sketch 194). That simply made the design fussy. Eventually, sketch 249 was chosen to be the archetypal mark, striking a healthy balance between heavy and light areas while maintaining a clockwise rotation.

I needed to investigate the typeface Baskerville with the emblem in place. When the master art was completed, I took the prototype to Will's apartment. Will propped the sketch upright on his dining room table and stood back to view it from a distance. He turned off some lights. Even in the dimly lit room it could be read very well. Will turned the lights back on.

"Resonate?" I offered.

"It resonates." Will was pleased. I was pleased.

Functional Requirements

REGARDLESS OF what kind of mark it is, all logos share a set of functional requirements. A logo must be seen in many circumstances, many of them unpredictable and uncontrollable. It must be useful for a period of time that can vary from a matter of days to a span of decades. Adaptable to a variety of materials, the logo must, in every situation, trigger in the public's mind correct identification as well as positive connotations.

These requirements can be divided into two types. One group of requirements has to do with the ability of a mark to be seen and remembered. We'll call these *alpha* demands. Another group of requirements has to do with the linking of the mark to the host and the communicated attitudes and feelings that accompany that linkage. We'll call these *omega* demands.

Alpha Demands: The need to be remembered

Alpha demands are about getting the public to recognize a mark. Think of your brain as a post office. When you see something that is striking or if you see something repeatedly, pathways are constructed between cells that, in effect, create a kind of post office box for that visual entity. Distinctive features, especially those seen repeatedly, get more mail. Recognizable faces, for example, owe their familiarity to the fact that memories are stored in a very large mailbox. When the face is seen again,

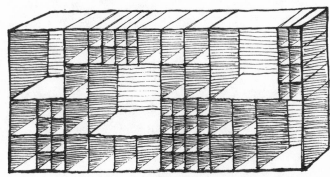

the new perception is sent to the mailbox where it connects with the memories stored there. One wants the host to have as large a mental mailbox as possible because then, as the visible front for the host, the mark becomes familiar. The ability of a visual mark to reach the memory center and claim a mailbox is called *penetration*. It's not easy to do. The world is full of other stimuli competing for those few slots. To succeed, the mark must do four things.

A mark must be visible—If it is to make an impression, a mark first must be seen. A new mark must compete with thousands of other visual symbols every day to win a viewer's attention. Even when it attracts the eye, a viewer can be expected to spend only three-tenths of a second glancing at it.

Keep in mind a few strategies when you work on this daunting task. Keep the logo distinct from any background clutter. Sometimes it is possible to control the limited region around the mark (a sign panel, a sheet of paper in the case of a letterhead, etc.), but the larger environment is often chaotic and changing. Therefore, change the appearance of a mark as little as possible. If you can predict how and when the background will compete with the mark, then you can design a mark with contrasting features.

Of course, big things, bright things and things in your line of sight are more visible than small, dull, peripheral objects. No matter how interesting a mark might be after it is spotted, it is important to consider if it has the power to attract attention to itself. If it cannot do that, then it may never have the chance to convey its aesthetic qualities.

One of the most successful techniques of camouflaging involves painting a large object with bright colors. How can a big, bright thing be made invisible? The colors are applied in geometric shapes that break the object into unrelated parts so that it cannot be seen as a whole unit. The lesson, in terms of enhancing visibility, is to attempt the opposite: create a mark that appears to be a *related*

whole even though it may be composed of different parts, thus creating a whole that is greater than the sum of its parts.

Sometimes, you can design a mark that plays some kind of visual game, an optical illusion perhaps, that arrests the viewer's gaze. You may be able to attain as much as a second of gaze time. In the chaotic urban visual environment, a second is a very long time. All the while, the viewer records the mark in memory.

A mark must be recognizable—Visible marks are not always recognizable marks. Recognition means that the mark will be recalled when a viewer sees it again. The feature that arrests a viewer's gaze may function like the hook of a pop song, engaging the viewer's mind, staying there in short-term memory after the gaze has passed on. The second time the mark is viewed, that memory seed blossoms into recognition: "I've seen that face before." If a mark is recognized, then there is proof that it has penetrated.

Anything that is visually intriguing will help a mark be recognized. The intrigue can derive from the subject content of the mark or it can derive from the form of the mark. In either case, the mark must have some quality that sets it apart from other things, some aspect that makes it unique.

A mark must be memorable—If recognition is the awareness of familiarity when seeing a mark that has been seen before, a memorable mark is one that can be recalled even when not being viewed. It has the power to stay in the mind as an independent, recallable idea.

A mark may be memorable simply because the kind of visual game it plays is so effective that it penetrates very deeply at first sight. It may be memorable because it has been repeated so often that it becomes a familiar part of the environment. Either way, memorability is a great asset for the host and one of the highest goals to set for the design of a mark.

A mark must be versatile—When you create a mark, you cannot envision every possible use for it. Therefore, it is important that the mark be versatile so that it can be treated in any material, at any size, in any environment, and still be functional. Large companies that may need to apply their logo in countless ways (such as letterhead, packaging, etc.) will need this versatility especially.

Ask yourself, can the mark be sewn? Can it be etched in glass? Stamped in wood? Embossed? How does it look on television with a snowy picture? A computer monitor? Can it withstand being printed in a small size on newsprint? Does it work as effectively in black and white as in color? The goal is to present your client with a mark that not only is successful in the presentation but also functions in the real world.

Omega Demands: Linkage to the host

Alpha demands are about logo recognition. Omega demands ensure that the logo is linked to the host and carries with it appropriate connotations. There are three omega demands.

The mark must identify the host—

The most basic aspect of linkage is that the logo identify the host. You may see a mark and recognize it as one you've seen before, even find it compelling and memorable, yet you have no notion what it identifies. A successful logo must establish a clear identifying link, or it functions simply as a pretty picture, nonsensical sign or, what is worse, misidentification.

It is not necessary that this identification happen at first viewing. For example, an ideograph by its abstract nature is ineffective as an identifier on first viewing, but the public can be taught to make the connection. After the connection is made, the ideograph may work very well.

The mark must be classified correctly—When a logo penetrates the memory of a viewer, it enters a realm of message and memory linkages. It becomes part of a web of interconnected meanings, associations and categories that is complex, always changing, influencing and being influenced by new perceptions. This pulsating network of connected mental influences is a process of sign exchange called *semiosis*.

The visual form of the logo will remind the viewer of other logos. Each viewer will bring many associations to the mark that simply cannot be predicted or controlled, because they arise from each individual's unique experience. These relationships that the viewer brings to the mark are called *connotations*. Even though all connotations cannot be predicted or controlled, a mark can be planned in such a way that most of the targeted audience can be expected to bring a defined cluster of interpretation to it.

Aspects of a mark that are intended to work by connotation are called subcodes. Based on common but undefined usage, subcodes often work subliminally when viewed by the public. They work by association with things commonly seen, but not explicitly set forth. Once I was working on a project for a company involved in the automobile service industry. The former mark had been a logotype based on the typeface Benguiat, a typeface that has exaggerated thin parts and is fairly tall and narrow. It was important to suggest the automobile industry in the new mark. Studying the proportions used in the logotypes of tire and car manufacturers, it became clear that most of these logos were expanded (horizontally) and that they were bold. By designing the mark to be bold and extended, the logo was not only correctly identified, but it was also properly classified as a participant in the auto industry.

The mark must express the appropriate attitude—The form of the mark can trigger an emotional response. This "attitude" that the mark carries is unmistakable, but is referred to by several terms: mood, tone, style, feel, etc. This emotional response is very real and fairly constant within a given culture. The mood of your mark is a subjective issue, but one that must be put into words. It is at the heart of the design process. Try to discuss the mood of the mark with your client. It is necessary that this feeling be appropriate to the host. Successful marks are expressive, and that expression is appropriate to the profile of the host.

The confidence in mark 244 is reflected in a more precise and careful drawing style. While the mark appears fresh and energetic, it does have the unfortunate characteristic of appearing to have a propeller through the center. This apparition eventually becomes so distracting that even after putting it aside for a few days it is necessary to change the mark somehow to eliminate the propeller.

Sketch 245 changes the progression so that the center of the mark rests in a vacant area instead of on a wave. In this way the propeller is eliminated. The white stripe that flows through the mark is a suitable counterpart to the undulating waves.

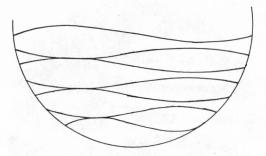

Three armatures were carefully drawn, each
testing a different amount of overlap in the way the
waves blended. Sketch 246 tends to produce a light
weight symbol; sketch 247 is crisp and clear. Sketch
248 yields a darker symbol (sketch 249), with more
stress to the spinning black areas.

Sketches 248(31.C19)

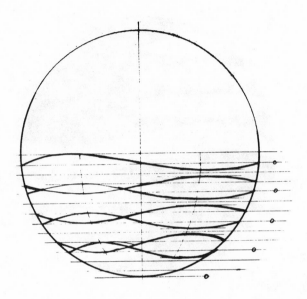

Sketches 249(31.C20)

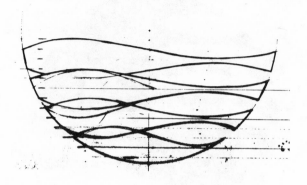

Sketch 250 gives a much darker symbol with the white lozenges appearing to be figures against the dark background disk.

The white center stripe in version 247 seems to be of a different style than the rest of the mark because it doesn't change in thickness. Sketch 249 shows how this stripe is softened by adding fins at the outermost edges. With that addition, the central stripe

seems more in keeping with the other features.

These explorations show that when the black areas become too thick, the movement of the mark is diminished and the waveform becomes less obvious. On the other hand, if too much light is let into the mark, it becomes weak. Sketch 249 seems to strike a balance. It has good movement, a balance of light and dark, and a well-articulated outer edge. All that is left is

to investigate the perfect balance of thickness of the white lozenges and the central stripe. These features should be in a unified relation to one another. This balance cannot be accomplished by measurement because the center stripe is much longer and straighter than the lozenges. Sketches 252 and 253 proved that very small changes to the shape of the waves caused quite a bit of difference in the thickness of the center

stripe. Sketch 249 was chosen to be the basic design. The mark must now be drawn larger and more carefully so that the details can be worked out.

117

Sketches 254–262: Refinement evolves into master art. Sketch 254 is illustrated actual size. I had assumed that the curves were arcs and could easily be drawn with a compass. Instead, careful study of the curves showed that they were not portions of circles, but slightly parabolic in shape. This necessitated drawing them freehand. Whether drawn on a computer or manually, this is no easy task. In this case, sketch 254 was used as a refined freehand drawing. Then it was reproduced at 200 percent and cleaned up. Finally, two duplicates were made and pasted together to form one whole disk. That composite comprised the master art for the emblem.

I had planned to use Baskerville as the type-face for the logotype. But when I placed the Baskerville B, I and S next to the newly mastered emblem, I found that the details lacked similarity. Baskerville seemed too squat and the serifs were too blunt. I thought I might be able to add more relationships between type and emblem if some of the details in the waves were picked up in the letterforms.

Sketch 255: This is a reproduction showing how the B was drawn. If you look carefully at the texture of the paper, you will notice areas where white opaquing has been used to correct the drawing. Each of the letters was drawn and corrected in this manner. The illustration is actual size. I drew the letters free-hand with black ink and plaka on drafting vellum.

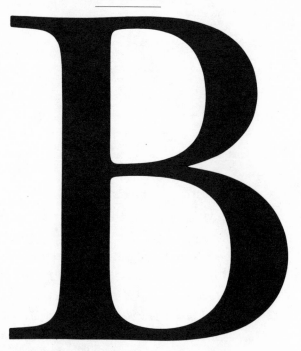

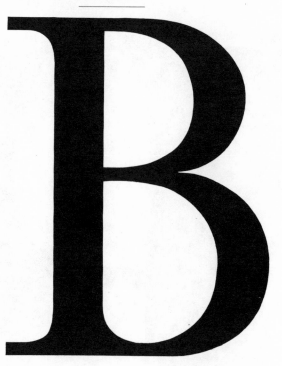

Sketches 256–261: These drawings compare the form of the Baskerville letterforms with the drawn characters for BIOS. The first letters of each set are the BIOS letterforms. Notice the sharper serifs, especially in the S, and how they relate to the endings of the waveforms in the emblem.

BIOS

Sketch 262: The prototype BIOS logo, complete.

Epilogue

TWO MONTHS had passed since work on BIOS had begun. Busy packing for a summer in Italy, I employed an assistant to help with the final production work necessary for application of the mark to stationery and all the other venues that give a mark life.

Will would oversee the printing of the items while I was in Italy. He would, in a sense, be present for the birth of the BIOS mark. For me, the birth is anticlimactic. It is the gestation period that is exciting: reaching for the archetype is the core of the game. One feels, in this work, a primal struggle that is at the heart of our need to communicate. It is a game that requires total concentration and complete engagement, a game that never is dull. My last words to Will LaValley were to thank him for the opportunity to solve such an interesting problem. We had each learned a great deal, and we had not used a Mobius strip or yin-yang after all.

Appendix
Protocol Diagram

Series 1	Series 2	Series 3		Series 4	
Sketch 001(1.1)	Sketch 010(2.1)	Sketch 011(3.1)		Sketch 047(4.1)	
Sketch 002(1.2)		Sketch 012(3.2)		Sketch 048(4.2)	
Sketch 003(1.3)		Sketch 013(3.3)		Sketch 049(4.3)	
Sketch 004(1.4)		Sketch 014(3.4)		Sketch 050(4.4)	
Sketch 005(1.5)		Sketch 015(3.5)		Sketch 051(4.5)	
Sketch 006(1.6)		Sketch 016(3.6)		Sketch 052(4.6)	
Sketch 007(1.7)		Sketch 017(3.7)		Sketch 053(4A.7)	Sketch 065(4B.7)
Sketch 008(1.8)		Sketch 018(3.8)		Sketch 054(4A.8)	Sketch 066(4B.8)
Sketch 009(1.9)		Sketch 019(3.9)		Sketch 055(4A.9)	Sketch 067(4B.9)
		Sketch 020(3.10)		Sketch 056(4A.10)	Sketch 068(4B.10)
		Sketch 021(3.11)		Sketch 057(4A.11)	Sketch 069(4B.11)
		Sketch 022(3.12)		Sketch 058(4A.12)	Sketch 070(4B.12)
		Sketch 023(3.13)		Sketch 059(4A.13)	Sketch 071(4B.13)
		Sketch 024(3.14)		Sketch 060(4A.14)	Sketch 072(4B.14)
		Sketch 025(3.15)		Sketch 061(4A.15)	Sketch 073(4B.15)
		Sketch 026(3A.16)	Sketch 027(3B.16)	Sketch 062(4A.16)	Sketch 074(4B.16)
		Sketch 028(3A.17)	Sketch 029(3B.17)	Sketch 063(4A.17)	Sketch 075(4B.17)
		Sketch 040(3A.18)	Sketch 030(3B.18)	Sketch 064(4A.18)	Sketch 076(4B.18)
		Sketch 041(3A.19)	Sketch 031(3B.19)		Sketch 077(4B.19)
		Sketch 042(3A.20)	Sketch 032(3B.20)		
			Sketch 033(3B.21)		
			Sketch 034(3B.22)		
			Sketch 035(3B.23)		
			Sketch 036(3B.24)		
			Sketch 037(3B.25)		
			Sketch 038(3B.26)		
			Sketch 039(3B.27)		
			Sketch 043(3B.28)		
			Sketch 044(3B.29)		
			Sketch 045(3B.30)		
			Sketch 046(3B.31)		

Series 5	**Series 6**	**Series 7**	**Series 8**
Sketch 078(5.1)	Sketch 079(6.1)	Sketch 080(7.1)	Sketch 081(8.1)

Series 9	**Series 10**	**Series 11**
Sketch 082(9.1)	Sketch 083(10.1)	Sketch 084(11.1)

Series 12

Sketch 085(12.1)
Sketch 086(12.2)
Sketch 087(12.3)
Sketch 088(12.4)
Sketch 102(12.5)
Sketch 103(12.6)
Sketch 104(12.7)
Sketch 105(12.8)
Sketch 106(12.9)
Sketch 107(12.10)
Sketch 108(12.11)
Sketch 109(12.12)
Sketch 110(12.13)
Sketch 111(12.14)
Sketch 112(12.15)
Sketch 113(12.16)
Sketch 114(12.17)
Sketch 115(12.18)
Sketch 116(12.19)

Sketch 118(12.A20)	Sketch 117(12.B20)	Sketch 135(12.C20)	Sketch 141(12.D20)	Sketch 144(12.E20)
Sketch 119(12.A21)			Sketch 140(12.D21)	Sketch 145(12.E21)
Sketch 120(12.A22)			Sketch 137(12.D22)	Sketch 146(12.E22)
Sketch 121(12.A23)			Sketch 136(12.D23)	
Sketch 122(12.A24)			Sketch 138(12.D24)	
Sketch 123(12.A25)			Sketch 139(12.D25)	
Sketch 124(12.A26)			Sketch 142(12.D26)	
Sketch 125(12.A27)			Sketch 143(12.D27)	

Series 23

Sketch 165(23.1)

Series 24

Sketch 166(24.1)

Sketch 167(24.A2)   Sketch 169(24.B2)
Sketch 168(24.A3)   Sketch 170(24.B3)
                           Sketch 171(24.B4)
                           Sketch 172(24.B5)
                           Sketch 173(24.B6)

Series 25

Sketch 174(25.1)